ᕿᑯᕐᖓ

ᑕᓪᓕᒪᓂ ᐅᖅᑲᓇᐃᓴᐊᖅᑕᖏᓂ:

Cover Illustration: © Ben Shannnon

ᖃᓄᖅ ᐃᓄᐃᑦ
ᐅᖃᐅᓯᖃᖅᓯᒪᕙᑦ ᒥᒃᓵᓄᑦ

ᐃᖃᓗᒡᔪᐊᑉ ᒥᒃᓵᓄᑦ?

ᓇᑭᖕᒫᖅᓯᒪᓂᖓ: Chondrichthyes
(ᖃᖅᑯᐊᓛᑦ ᐃᖃᓗᖅ)
ᖃᓄᐃᕐᑑᓂᖓ: Somniosus microcephalus
ᑕᑭᓂᖓ: 2.5 to 7.3 m
ᐅᖁᒪᐃᓐᓂᖓ:
ᑎᑭᐅᑎᔪᓐᓇᖅᑐᖅ
1,2000 kg

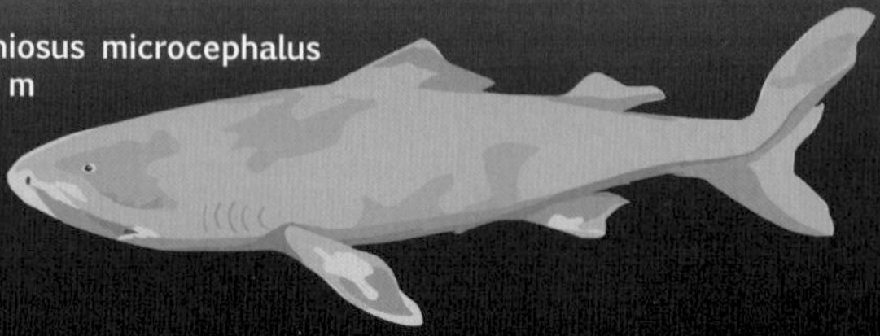

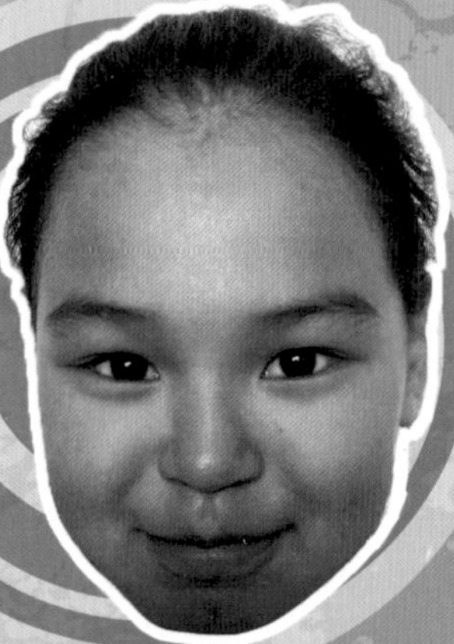

“ᑭᒍᑎᓕᒃ
ᒥᑭᖅᑑᑎᑯᓗᙱᒃ
ᐅᖅᓱᓕᐊᓘᑦᓗᓂ.”
ᐋᔅᑕ ᕼᐅᑲᓇᒃ,
ᖁᕐᓗᖅᑐᖅ

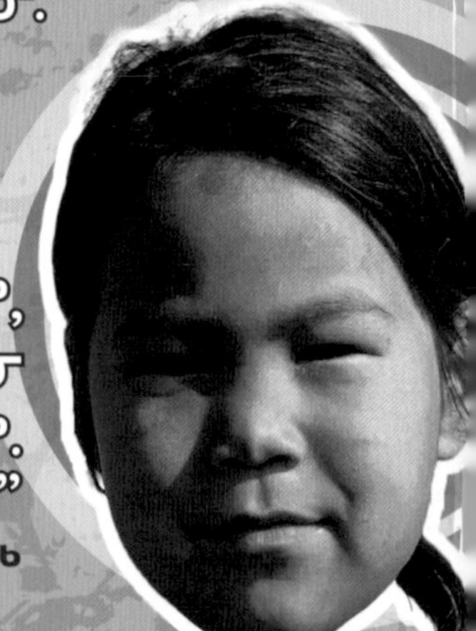

“ᐃᖃᓗᐊᓘᔮᖅᑐᖅ,
ᑭᓯᐊᓂ
ᑲᐸᐊᓇᖅᓯᖅᓴᖅ.
ᐃᖅᓯᓇᕈᓇᖅᑐᐊᓗᒃ.”
ᐅᒃᐱᒃ ᖃᔭᖅᑳᖅ, ᑰᒑᕐᔪᒃ

“ᐊᖏᔪᐊᓗᐃᑦ ᐱᑐᖄᓘᔪᓐᓇᖅᑐᑦ.
ᐊᒥᓱᐊᓗᙱᓪᓗ ᐃᐱᒃᑐᐊᓗᙱᒃ
ᑭᒍᑎᖃᕈᓐᓇᖅᑐᑎᒃ.”
ᐃᐅᕆᐅᑦ ᑎᐊᓯᕇ ᐃᑎᒪᖕᓇᒃ, ᑰᒑᕐᔪᒃ

ᐅᖃᐅᓯᕐᔪᐊᑦ

— ᔅᐃᐃᓕᓐ ᐊᕐᓇᒃᖅ.

ᐃᖃᓗᒍᔭᕐᐊᑦ ᐊᑯᓂᐊᓗᒃ
ᐅᒪᕐᓇᖅᑐᖦᐆᖅᕣᓇᒪᓐᐅᔪᐊᖅᑐᓂᒃ
ᐊᕐᚡᔪᓂᒃ. ᐅᖃᖅᑐᖅᖅᕦᒥᔭᖅ
ᐅᒪᕐᓇᖅᑐᖦᐅᕐᐆᒃ ᐃᖢᖅᖏᕐᑕᒍᑦ
ᑐᖁᑕᐅᑉᑎᑐᐊᖅᕝᕈᑦ. ᑐᖁᑕᐅᔾᖂᓐᑕ,
ᐊᖦᒐᖏᕐᒃ ᐊᐃᑕᖅᕦᑉᒪᖅᑐᑦ
ᓂᕐᒐᒃ ᐊᐃᑐᖅᖘᑕᐅᕝᕈᑕ,
ᓂᐊᖅᑐᐊᖅᖘᒥᓐᓐᒍᐊᖅᑎᓪᒍᓐᒃ.

ᐃᖃᓗᒡᔪᐊᑦ: ᖃᐅᔨᒪᓇᖏᑦᑐᖅ “ᓯᓂᒃᑎ ᐃᖃᓗᒡᔪᐊᖅ”!

ᐃᖃᓗᒡᔪᐊᑦ ᐃᒪᕙᖕᒦᓲᑦ ᕿᑭᖅᑖᓘᑉ ᐃᒪᖓᓂ ᑲᓛᓖᑦ ᓄᓇᖓᑕ ᐃᑭᖕᒐᓂᒃ ᐊᐃᔅᓚᓐᑐ, ᑕᑯᔭᐅᓯᒪᖕᒥᔪᑦ ᓴᑦᑎᑦᑐᒥ ᐊᒡᓛᑦ ᕗᓗᐊᕆᑕᐅᑉ ᐃᒪᖓᓂ ᐃᒪᖕᒐ ᓈᒻᒪᒃᑎᓪᓗᒍ. ᐃᑎᔪᐊᓗᖕᒥᐅᑕᐅᓰᑦ, ᓂᒡᓚᓱᒃᑐᐊᓗᖕᓂᒃ (ᑎᑭᑦᑐᒍ 2,774 ᒦᑐᓂᒃ ᐃᑎᓂᓕᖕᒥ) ᑕᑯᔭᐅᓚᔪᐃᑦᑐᑎᒃᓗ.

ᐱᓇᓱᒃᑎᑦ

ᐃᖃᓗᒡᔪᐊᑦ ᐱᓇᓱᒃᑎᖃᙱᓚᑦ ᖃᐅᔨᒪᔭᐅᔪᓂᒃ ᐃᓄᐃᑦ ᐊᓯᖕᒋᓐᓂᒃ.

ᐱᐊᕋᖕᒋᑦ

ᐃᖃᓗᒡᔪᐊᑦ ᐱᐊᕋᖕᒋᑦ ᒪᓐᓂᐅᓲᖑᙹᑦ ᐊᖅᓇᖕᒋᑕ ᐃᓗᐊᓂ ᐃᖅᓂᓇᓲᖕᓂᖕᒋᓐᓂᒃ. ᐊᑕᐅᑦᑎᒃᑯᑦ 10-ᓂᒃ ᐃᖅᓂᓲᖑᙹᑦ. ᐃᖃᓗᒡᔪᐊᑦ ᐱᐊᕋᖕᒋᑦ ᖃᓪᓗᓈᑎᑐᑦ ᑕᐃᔭᐅᙹᑦ “ᐸᑉ”-ᓂᒃ.

ᓂᕿᖕᒋᑦ

ᐃᖃᓗᒡᔪᐊᑦ ᑭᓯᕈᓗᑐᐃᓐᓇᑦᑎᐊᓂᒃ ᓂᕿᖅᑲᓲᖕᒍᓂᖕᒋᓐᓂᒃ ᖃᐅᔨᒪᔭᐅᙹᑦ! ᐃᒃᓯᓐᓇᑯᓂᒃ ᓂᕆᓲᖑᓂᖕᒋᓐᓂᒃ ᖃᐅᔨᒪᔭᐅᒻᒥᔪᑦ, ᐆᒪᔪᕙᓂᖅᓂᒃ ᐊᖅᑰᓴᖅᑕᖕᒋᓐᓂᒃ ᓂᕆᓲᑦ-ᓲᖅᓗ ᓇᑦᑎᕙᓃᑦ, ᐃᖃᓗᕙᓃᑦ, ᓇᓄᕙᓃᑦᓗ ᑐᒃᑐᕙᓃᑦᓗ.

ᐊᖏᓂᖓ

ᐃᖃᓗᒡᔪᐊᑦ ᐊᖏᔪᐊᓗᐃᑫ! ᐅᖁᒪᐃᓐᓂᖃᕈᓐᓇᖅᑐᑦ 1,200 ᑭᓗᒍᙵᓂᒃ ᑕᑭᓂᖃᕐᓗᑎᒡᓗ 7.3 ᒦᑐᓂᒃ. ᓇᓗᓇᐃᖅᓱᔾᔪᑎᒋᓗᒍ, 1,200 ᑭᓗᒍᙵ ᐅᖁᒪᐃᑎᒋᔪᖅ 15 ᐃᓐᓇᐃᑦ ᐊᖒᑎᑎᑐᑫ! ᐊᖏᓛᖅ ᖄᖅᑖᓗᒃ ᐃᖃᓗᒡᔪᐊᖅ ᐊᖏᓂᖅᓴᐅᔪᖅ ᐃᖃᓗᒡᔪᐊᒥᑦ.

ᓲᒃᑲᓕᓂᖓ

ᐃᖃᓗᒡᔪᐊᑦ ᓲᒃᑲᓕᔪᐊᓘᔪᓐᓇᖅᑐᑦ-ᓲᒃᑲᐃᑦᑐᐊᓗᐃᑦ. ᐳᐃᒥᒍᓐᓇᖅᑐᑦ 1.22 ᑭᓛᒥᑐᓂᒃ ᐃᑲᕐᕿᒥ, ᓲᒃᑲᓂᖅᐹᖓᓕ 3.6 ᑭᓛᒥᑐ ᐃᑲᕐᕿᒥ. ᖄᖅᑖᓗᒡᓕ ᐃᖃᓗᒡᔪᐊᖅ ᓲᒃᑲᓂᖅᐹᖓ ᖃᐅᔾᔭᐅᓯᒪᔪᖅ 40 ᑭᓛᒥᑐᓂᒃ ᓲᒃᑲᓂᖅᑲᖅᑎᓪᓗᒍ ᐃᑲᕐᕿᒥ, ᖃᐅᔾᔮᔭᖅᐸᑦ ᖃᓄᑎᒋ ᓲᒃᑲᐃᑎᒋᒪᖔᑦ ᐃᖃᓗᒡᔪᐊᖅ. ᖃᐅᔾᔨᒪᔭᖅ, ᐃᖃᓗᒡᔪᐊᖅ ᓲᒃᑲᐃᓛᕐᒥ ᐳᐃᒥᓲᖑᓂᖓᓂᑦ ᐊᖏᓂᖅᑲᖅᑎᓪᓗᒍ ᑕᐃᒫᒃ ᐃᖃᓗᒃ. ᖃᐅᔨᒪᔭᐅᔾᔪᑎᒋᕚ ᕿᑐᖕᓂᖓᓄᑦ ᑕᐃᔭᐅᔾᔪᑎᒋᒃᑲᓐᓂᓕᖅᐹ "ᓯᓂᒃᑎ ᐃᖃᓗᒡᔪᐊᖅ."

ᑕᒃᐱᖕᓂᖓ

ᐃᖃᓗᒡᔪᐊᑦ ᑕᐅᑐᙱᐸᓗᒃᑐᑦ. ᐃᔨᖏᑦᑎᒍᑦ ᑯᒥᓵᖑᒪᓚᑕ, ᐃᔨᖏᓪᓗ ᓱᖅᑐᑎᒃ (ᐃᔨᖓᑕ ᖄᖓ), ᑕᐅᑦᑎᐊᕈᓐᓃᕈᑎᒋᓪᓗᒋᓪᓗ. ᑖᓐᓇ ᐊᑲᐃᓪᓕᐅᕈᑕᐅᙱᓚᖅ ᐃᖃᓗᒡᔪᐊᖑᑦ. ᖃᐅᒪᓂᖅ ᑎᑭᐅᒪᔪᓐᓇᖏᓪᒪᑦ ᐃᑎᔪᒥ ᓇᔪᖅᐸᑦᑕᖓᓐᓄᑦ, ᑕᒃᐱᖕᓂᖅ ᐊᑑᑎᖃᖏᑦᑐᖅ ᐊᖑᓇᓱᐊᖅᑕᒥᓂᒃ ᐊᖑᕖᒃᑕᖏᓐᓄᑦ. ᐃᖃᓗᒡᔪᐊᓪᓕ ᖃᐅᔾᔪᑎᒋᕖᒃᑕᖏᓐᓂᒃ ᐊᓱᖏᓐᓂᒃ ᐊᑐᓲᖑᔫᑦ. ᖃᐅᔾᔮᖅᑎᓪᓕ ᐃᓯᒪᔫᑦ ᐃᔨᖏᓐᓃᓲᑦ ᑯᒪᑦ ᐱᐅᒋᔭᐅᓲᖑᓯᓇᓪᓗᒋᑦ ᐊᖑᓇᓱᒃᐸᒃᑕᖏᓐᓄᑦ ᐃᖃᓗᒡᔪᐊᐸ. ᑯᒪᑦ ᐃᖃᓗᒡᔪᐊᐸ ᐃᔨᖏᓐᓃᓲᑦ ᖃᐅᒪᓲᖑᓯᓇᔭᐅᔫᑦ (ᖃᐅᒻᒪᓲᑦ); ᑕᐃᒫᒃ ᐆᒪᔪᑦ ᐃᖃᓗᒡᔪᐊᖑᖅᐸᓪᓕᐊᓲᖑᓯᓇᔭᐅᔫᑦ.

ᐆᒪᔪᓐᓇᕐᓂᖏᑦ

ᐃᖃᓗᒡᔪᐊᖅ ᕿᒥᕐᓗᓕᖕᓂᒃ ᐊᑯᓂᐅᓂᖅᐹᖅ ᐆᒪᓲᖅ ᓄᓇᕐᔪᐊᒥ. ᐆᒻᔪᓐᓇᖅᑐᖅ ᑎᑭᐅᑎᓗᒍ 272 ᐊᕐᕌᒍᑦ, ᐊᓛᑦ ᑎᑭᐅᑎᓗᒍ 500 ᐊᕐᕌᒍᑦ. ᓲᖃᐃᓪᓗ ᐃᖃᓗᒡᔪᐊᑦ ᓇᓗᓇᐃᖅᑕᐅᓯᒪᔪᓄᑦ ᖃᖅᑯᐊᓂᒃ ᓴᐅᓂᓕᖓᓄᑦ ᐃᖃᓗᓄᑦ-ᐃᒪᕐᒥᐅᑕᓄᑦ ᐆᒪᔪᓄᑦ ᓴᐅᓂᒃᓴᕋᓗᐊᖏᑦ ᖃᖅᑯᐊᖏᓐᓇᐅᑎᓪᓗᒋᑦ-ᖃᐅᔨᒪᓇᙱᓕᑦᓕ ᐊᕐᕌᒍᓪᓚᓇᖏᑦ. ᖃᐅᔨᓴᖅᑎᓄᑦ ᓴᐅᓃᑦ ᖃᖅᑯᐊᓂᒃ ᖃᐅᔾᔭᕐᓂᓇᔭᐅᓂᖅᓴᐅᒪᑕ ᐊᕐᕌᒍᖏᓐᓂᒃ, ᑕᐃᒫᒃ ᖃᐅᔨᒪᙱᓕᖅ ᖃᔅᓯᓂᒃ ᐊᕐᕌᒍᖃᓪᓚᓇᖕᒪᖔᑕ ᐃᖃᓗᒡᔪᐊᑦ.

Illustration: © Dotted Yeti/Shutterstock.com

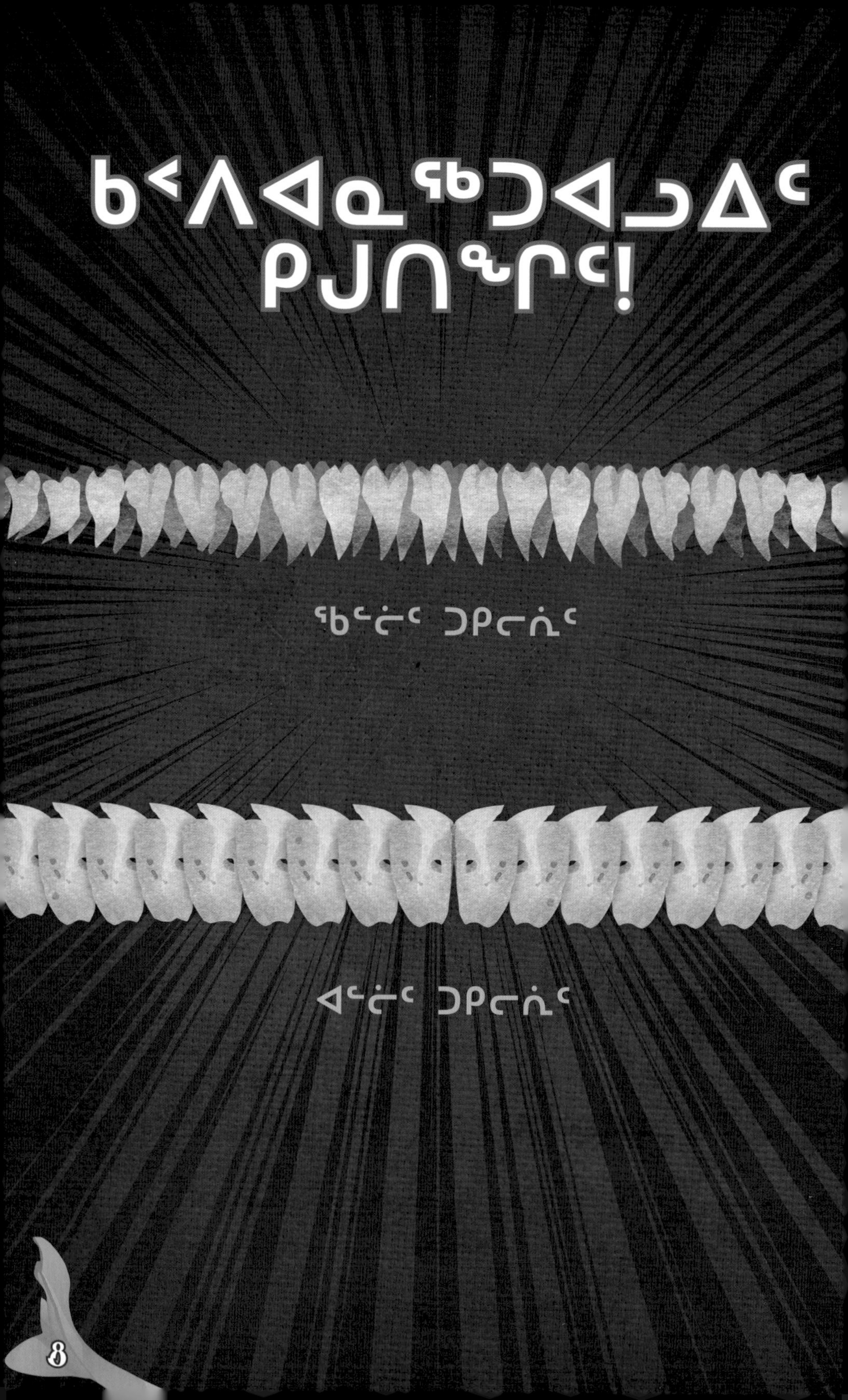
ᑲᑉᐱᐊᓇᖅᑐᐊᓗᐃᑦ
ᑭᒍᑎᖕᒋᑦ!
ᖃᓪᓛᑦ ᑐᑭᓕᓃᑦ
ᐊᓪᓛᑦ ᑐᑭᓕᓃᑦ

ᐃᖃᓗᒡᔪᐊᑦ ᑭᒍᑎᖏᑦ ᑲᒪᓇᖅᑐᐊᓗᐃᑦ ᐃᖃᓗᒡᔪᐊᓄᑦ. ᖁᓪᓘᑦ ᑭᒍᑎᖏᑦ 48-52 ᓄᕗᓕᐊᓗᐃᑦ, ᓵᑦᑐᒍᓗᐃᑦ, ᐊᓪᓛᓪᓕ ᑕᐃᒫᑦᑕᐅᖅ ᐊᒥᓱᑎᕆᔪᑦ ᓴᓂᒧᒃᑭᐅᓂᖅᓴᑦ ᓯᓚᒻᒧᖓᓪᓗᑎᒃ. ᖁᓪᓘᑦ ᑭᒍᑎᖏᑦ ᐊᖑᔭᖏᓐᓂᒃ ᐱᓯᒪᒃᔪᑎᖏᑦ, ᐊᓪᓛᓪᓕ ᐃᓚᙵᓯᒃᔪᑎᖏᑦ ᓂᕿᓂᐊᖅᑕᒥᖕᓂᒃ. ᓂᕿᓂᐊᖅᑎᓪᓗᒋᑦ ᐃᖃᓗᒡᔪᐊᑦ ᓂᐊᖁᓂ ᐅᐃᔾᔭᖅᑎᓲᖏᑦ ᓂᕿᓕᕐᖓᑕ.

ᐃᓚᙵᓯᓇᓱᒃᑎᓪᓗᒋᑦ ᐊᖑᑕᒥᓂᒃ, ᐃᖃᓗᒡᔪᐊᓪᓕ ᓂᕿᔪᓐᓇᓲᖑᕗᑦ ᐆᒪᔪᕕᓂᖁᔪᐊᕌᓗᖕᓂᒃ ᐊᖏᓗᐊᕋᔭᖅᑐᓂᒃ ᐅᖁᒻᒥᕿᐊᒃᓴᖅ ᐃᓚᙶᑎᕿᓪᓗᑎᒃ-ᓱᖁᓗ ᓴᖅᐱᓕᕕᓂᖅᓂᒃ.

ᑭᒍᑎᖏᑦ ᐊᔾᔨᐅᖏᑦᑐᑦ ᖃᐅᔨᒪᔭᐅᔾᔪᑎᒋᕙᐃᑦ. ᓇᑦᑎᕕᓃᑦ ᐃᑭᓘᑦ ᐊᖓᓗᖅᑐᓂᒃ ᑎᒥᒥᒃᑎᒍᑦ ᑎᐱᔾᔮᐅᓯᒪᖃᑦᑕᓕᖅᑎᓪᓗᒋᑦ ᓴᐃᐳᓪ ᕿᑭᖅᑕᕐᒥ, ᓅᕙ ᓯᑰᓯᐊᒥ, ᖃᐅᔨᓇᓱᒃᑏᑦ ᖃᐅᔨᔪᒪᓕᓚᐅᖅᓯᒪᖕᒪᑦ ᑭᓱᐊᓗᒃ ᑲᐸᐊᓇᖅᑐᐊᓗᒃ ᑕᐃᒫᒃ ᐃᑭᑖᖅᑎᑦᑎᑦᑕᕐᓂᕐᒪᖔᑦ. ᐃᓚᖏᑦ ᐃᓄᐃᑦ—ᐊᒡᓛᑦ ᓈᓴᓄᑦ ᔮᐅᒍᕌᕕᒃ-ᒥ ᐊᔾᔨᓕᐅᓇᔾᑦ ᐊᑦᐆᓚᐅᖅᓯᒪᔪᑦ ᐃᖃᓗᒡᔪᐊᒥᒃ "ᓯᓖᖅᓯᑎᑐᑦ ᑐᖁᕋᐃᔾ." ᒦᓐᓇ ᓱᓕ ᐅᖃᓪᓚᐅᑕᐅᓲᖅ ᐃᖃᓗᒡᔪᐊ ᑕᐃᒪᐃᑎᑦᑎᓐᓂᕐᒪᖔᑦ, ᑭᓱᐊᓂ ᖃᐅᔨᒪᔭᐅᔪᖅ, ᑖᓐᓇ ᓱᒃᑲᐃᑦᑐᐊᓗᒃ ᐃᖃᓗᒡᔪᐊᖅ ᑕᑯᓕᒪᓇᖏᑦᑐᒥᒃ ᑮᓯᔾᔪᓯᓕᒃ!

ᐊᑑᑎᑐᖃᖕᒋᑦ ᐊᑑᑎᒋᓕᖅᑕᖕᒋᓪᓗ: ᐃᖃᓗᒡᔪᐊᑦ

“ᐃᖃᓗᒡᔪᐊᑦ ᑕᑯᔭᐅᒐᔪᖕᒋᑦᑐᑦ ᕿᑭᖅᑖᓘᑉ ᓂᒋᐊᓂ ᓄᓇᕗᒻᒥ, ᑭᓯᐊᓂ ᖁᑦᑎᑦᑐᕐᒨᖅᐸᓪᓕᐊᓪᓗᑎᑦ ᓄᓗᐊᖅᓯᒪᒐᔪᓕᓲᑦ.”
—ᐅᐃᓕᐊᒻ ᕝᓚᕼᐅᖅᑎ, ᐊᐅᓱᐃᑦᑐᖅ ᓄᓇᕗᑦ

ᖃᖅᑯᐊᑦ:

- ᐃᖃᓗᒡᔪᐊᑉ ᓴᐅᓂᖕᒋᑦ ᖃᖅᑯᐊᑦ, ᓴᐅᓂᐅᙱᑦᑐᑦ.
- ᐃᖃᓗᒡᔪᐊᑉ ᖃᖅᑯᐊᖕᒋᑦ ᐊᖅᓴᓕᐊᖑᕙᓚᐅᖅᓯᒪᔪᑦ ᓱᕋᓯᕐᓄᑦ ᑎᔾᔭᓪᓛᓲᖑᒻᒪᑕ.

Illustrations: Rebecca Brook

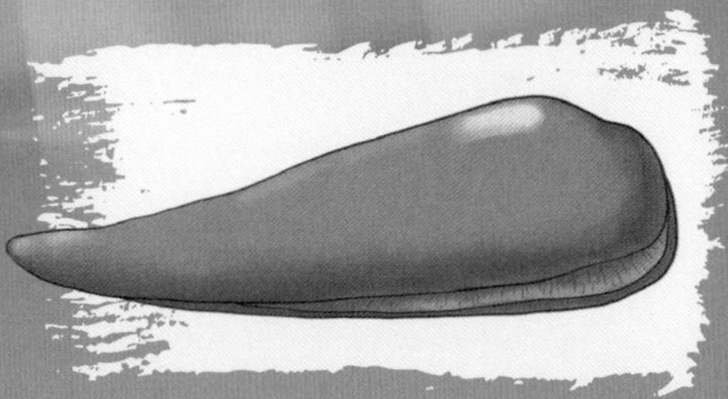

ᑎᖕᒍᖓ

· ᑲᓛᓛᑦ ᓄᓇᖓᓐᓂ ᐊᐃᔅᓚᓐᒥᓗ ᐃᖅᑲᓗᒡᔪᐊᑦ ᐃᖅᑲᓗᒐᓱᒃᑕᐅᕙᓚᐅᖅᓯᒪᔪᑦ ᑎᖕᒍᖕᒥᑕ ᐅᖅᓱᖕᒥᓐᓄᑦ, ᖃᐅᒻᒪᖅᑯᑎᖕᒥᓐᓄᑦ ᐅᖅᓯᓇᔭᐅᓂᐊᖅᒪᑕ.

· ᐱᒋᐊᓕᖅᑎᓪᓗᒋᑦ 20th ᓯᐊᓐᑐᕆ, ᐃᖅᑲᓗᒡᔪᐊᑦ ᐊᒥᓲᑎᒋᔪᑦ 50,000-ᓂᒃ ᐱᔭᐅᓚᐅᖅᓯᒪᔪᑦ ᑕᐃᒫᒃ ᐊᑑᑎᖅᑲᖅᓂᐊᖅᒪ ᐊᖅᕌᒍᒧᑦ.

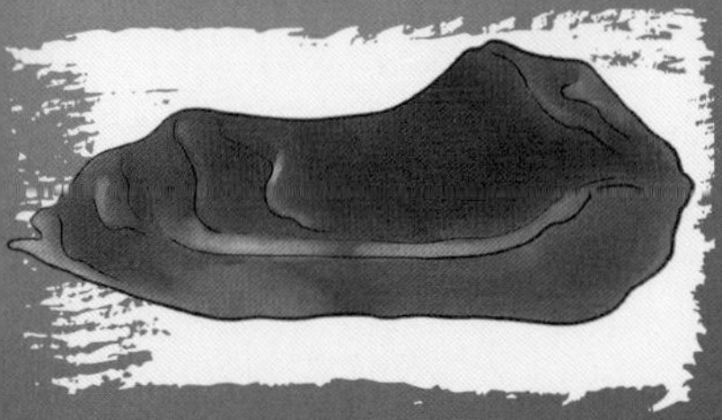

ᓂᖅᑭᖕᒋᑦ:

· ᕿᑭᖅᑖᓗᖕᒥ ᐃᖅᑲᓗᒡᔪᐊᑦ ᓂᖅᑭᒋᔭᐅᓲᖑᙱᑦᑐᑦ ᐃᖅᑲᓗᒐᓱᒃᑕᐅᓲᖑᓇᑎᒡᓗ.

· ᑲᓛᓛᓪᓚ ᓄᓇᖓᓐᓂ ᐃᖅᑲᓗᒐᓱᒃᑕᐅᓲᑦ ᓂᖅᑭᖕᒋᓪᓗ ᕿᒥᖅᑯᑎᒃᓴᓇᔭᐅᓪᓗᑎᒃ.

· ᐊᐃᔅᓚᓐᒥ ᐃᖅᑲᓗᒡᔪᐊᑦ ᓂᖅᑭᒋᔭᐅᔪᖅ! ᐃᖅᑲᓗᒡᔪᐊᕕᓃᑦ ᐃᒍᓇᖅᓯᐊᖑᓲᑦ ᓂᕕᖓᑎᑕᐅᓪᓗᑎᒃ ᑕᖅᑭᓂᒃ 4 ᐅᕝᕙᓘᓐᓃᑦ 5-ᓂᒃ. ᑕᐃᒫᒃ ᒪᒪᖅᑐᖅᑯᑎᒋᔭᐅᓲᖅ ᐊᐃᔅᓚᓐᒥ, ᑭᓯᐊᓂ ᑎᐱᒃᑭᐊᓗᐃᖅ!

ᐊᒪᐅᑕᓕᒃ

ᑎᑎᕋᖅᑐᖅ ᐊᒥᐊᖅ ᔪᐊᓱᐋ
ᑎᑎᖃᑐᓯᖅᑐᖅ ᔪᓕᓴ ᒍᐱ

ᐊᓚᐊᖅᑐᖅᑕᖅᑲᒐᓕᒃ ᑲᐸᐱᐊᖅᑐᓯᓐᑐ ᓄᐊ ᐃᒪᕐᓗ. ᓲᖅᑯᓪᓇ
ᐊᓚᐊᖅᑐᒐᑦ ᐃᓯᒃᕈᐅᓴᒐ ᐊᒪᐅᑕᓕᒃ. ᐊᖕᕐᔭᐊᒍᒃ, ᐊᖑᖐᒍᒃ
ᐃᓇᕐᑕᖕᕐᑐᐊᒍᒃ ᑎᑲᑎᐊᖕᖅ ᖅᑯᓪᐊᑎᓀᒃ ᓯᔭᖕᖑᒃ
ᓇᖕᒃᓇᑎᓗ ᐃᓇᐊᐅᐊᒃᖅᑐᓯᖕ ᐊᖕᕐᖅᐅᑎᓂᐊᕐᒐᕈ ᓂᕿᑎᕐᒐᓗᖕ.

ᐅᓪᓗᐃᑦ ᐃᓚᖓᓐᓂᑦ, ᐊᒪᐅᑕᓕᒃ ᓄᓇᒃᑯᑦ ᐱᓱᒃᑎᓪᓗᒍ.
ᕿᓂᖅᑐᓂ ᑭᓯᒥᒃᑭᐊᖅ, ᑭᓇᒥᓪᓘᓐᓃᒃᑭᐊᖅ, ᑳᒃᑐᐊᓘᒐᒥ.
ᑕᕝᕙᓕ, ᑐᓴᖅᑐᓂ ᐅᖃᓪᓚᕝᕙᓗᑦᑎᔪᓂᒃ ᑕᑯᓪᓗᓂᓗ
ᓱᕈᓰᖕᓂᒃ ᐃᓄᑑᓪᓗᑎᒃ ᐃᒃᓯᕚᖅᑑᖕᓂᒃ ᐃᓐᓇᖅᑕᖅᑲᕋᓂᓗ
ᖃᐅᔨᓴᖅᑐᓂᒃ.

ᓱᕈᓰᒃ ᐊᐃᑉᐸᖓ ᓄᑲᑉᐱᐊᖅ ᐊᐃᑉᐸᖓᓗ ᓂᕕᐊᖅᓯᐊᖅ.
ᓄᑲᑉᐱᐊᖅ ᐃᓕᐊᕐᔫᓪᓗᓂ ᓂᖏᐅᕐᒥᓂᒥᐅᑕᖅ. ᓲᖅᑲᐃᒻᒪ
ᐃᓕᐊᕐᔫᒐᒥ, ᐊᓐᓄᕌᖏᑦ ᒥᑭᑎᓕᖅᑕᐅᓂᑯᐃᓐᓇᐅᕙᒃᑐᑎᒃ.
ᓈᒪᑦᑎᐊᑯᓗᒍᓐᓇᕋᑎᒃ ᐊᓕᑦᑐᕐᓂᐅᕙᒃᑐᑎᒃᓗ.
ᐳᑐᒍᖓᓘᓐᓃᑦ ᐊᓃᖅᑐᓂ ᐳᔾᔪᖅᓯᒪᓗᐊᒧᑦ ᑲᒥᖏᒃ!

ᓂᓕᐊᖅᔪᐊᖅ ᓕᖕᒥᓂᒃᒥᑐᑕᐊᑎᐊᓕᐦᑐᓂᐸᑦ.
ᐱᓯᑎᐊᖅᖃᐅᒪᑦ ᓕᖃᑎᕐᒥᓕᐊᒃᓴᖅ ᖁᐃᓕᐊᑏᐦᑐᓂᐸᑦ
ᐅᑲᖕᖏᑦ ᑐᖕᓯᓂᖅᒐᑦᒐᓕᑕ. ᖁᑲᐸᓕᐊᖅ
ᑕᐸᔪᑕᖅᒐᑦᒐᓕᑕ ᓕᒻᒍᐊᓕᐦᖃᔪᑕᓕᑕᓗ
ᑭᑭᑕᐦᔨᓕᖁᕈᑐᓂ. ᖁᑲᐸᓕᐊᖅ ᐃᓇᖅᒃᖁᑐᓂ
ᐃᖄᐃᑦ ᐅᓇᖃᓕᓇᐦᓂᑕ, ᒐᖄᑎᓯᓂᓗ
ᐅᓇᖃᐅᑏᖅᑐᓂᐸᑦ ᓂᓕᐊᖅᔪᐊᖅ.

ᐅᓂᒃᖅᕭᑎᓕᖅᑐᒍ ᐊᒪᐅᑕᓕᖅᔪᒃ ᑎᓯᓕᐊᖅᑕᐅᓯᒪᔪᑏᑦ.
ᐊᒪᐅᑕᓕᖅᔪ ᖃᑕᓐᓪᖕᒪᑦ ᑎᒍᓯᔪᕐᖃᖅᓲᖅᓲᒐᓂ ᓯᒃᑯᒐᓈᓴ,
ᑕᖅᕋᑦᑯᑎᒋᑐ ᓯᒍᓵᒥᓄᑦ. ᓂᕕᐊᖅᓯᐊᖅ ᓄᖃᐸᓕᐊᕐᒍ
ᑕᑦᕕᖅᑐᑎᑉ.

ᐊᒪᐅᑕᕐᒃ ᐊᖕᑎᖄᔪᒃ ᖃᕙᓕᐊᓇᖅᑐᐊᒍᒃ
ᒪᒪᖕᕆᐅᑐᔪᐊᒍᒃ! ᓂᕕᐊᖅᓯᐊᖅ ᖃᕚᔅᓕᕐᒍᓂ ᐱᔭᐅᒍᓐ
ᓂᒃᔭᐅᓂᐊᕐᑦᓂᕐᒥᒥᒃ.

ᓄᑲᑉᐱᐊᖅ ᑲᑉᐱᐊᓱᒃᑐᓂ, ᑭᓯᐊᓂ ᐃᓱᒪᑦᓘᓂ ᓱᓂᐊᓕᕐᓂᕐᒥᓂᒃ. ᐸᖅᑭᔾᔮᕐᖃᖏᓐᓇᒥᓕ ᐅᓐᓃᑦ, ᓄᑲᑉᐱᐊᖅ ᐃᓱᒪᔭᕆᐊᖅᑲᓲᖑᒻᒪᑦ ᖄᓄᖅ ᐊᓂᒍᐃᓂᐊᕐᒪᖖᕈᕐᒥ ᐊᑐᖅᑕᒥᓂᒃ.

"ᓴᓴᓴᓴᓴᓴ," ᐅᖃᖅᑐᓂ ᓄᑲᑉᐱᐊᖅ. ᑎᒃᑯᐊᖅᑐᓂᐅᒡᓗ ᐳᑐᒍᓂ ᓄᐃᓴᐹᖅ ᐳᔾᐹᕐᓂᕐᒥᑎᒍᑦ ᑲᒥᒻᒥ. "ᓴᓴᓴ," ᐅᖃᒃᑲᓐᓂᖅᐳᖅ, "ᑐᐹᕐᓂᐊᖅᑕᐃᑦ."

ᐊᒫᑕᓕᒃ ᑕᑯᓚᐅᖅᓯᒪᖏᓐᓇᒥ ᓱᐳᓯᕐᒥᒃ ᑲᑉᐱᐊᓱᖏᑦᑐᒥᒃ ᑖᒃᓯᒥᖓ. ᓇᓗᓕᖅᑐᓂ, ᑕᑯᓐᓇᖅᑐᓂᐅᒃ ᐳᑐᒍᐊ ᐊᐅᓚᔾᔪᖅ. ᐊᐱᕆᓪᖁᖅ, "ᑭᓲᒪᑦ?"

ᓄᑲᑉᐱᐊᑉ ᐳᑐᒍᓂ ᐊᐅᓚᑏᓐᓇᖅᑐᓂᐅᒃ. “ᔅᔅᔅᔅ, ᐅᓇ ᐊᓂᐊᓇᖅᑐᖅ,” ᐅᖃᖅᐳᖅ.

“ᑭᓱᓂᒃ ᐊᓂᐊᓇᖅᑐᖅ ᓂᕆᓲᖑᒻᒪᑦ?” ᐊᒪᐅᑕᓂᒃ ᐊᐱᕆᒍᖅ, ᐱᖏᑲᑦᑑᔫᖅᑐᓂ.

“ᐆᒥᖓ ᐊᓂᐊᓇᖅᑐᒥᒃ,” ᓄᑲᑉᐱᐊᖅ ᐅᖃᖅᐳᖅ, “ᓂᕆᓲᖅ ᐊᒪᐅᑕᓂᖕᒥᒃ!”

ᐊᒪᐅᑕᓂᓪᓗ ᐅᑎᕆᐊᒐᓛᒃᐳᖅ. “ᐅᕙᓐᓅᖅᑎᑦᑕᐃᓂᐅᒃ!” ᖃᐃᒐᓪᓚᒃᐳᖅ ᕿᒫᓪᓗᓂᓗ.

ᐃᖃᓗᒡᔪᐊᑉ ᒥᒃᓵᓄᑦ ᐅᒃᐱᓇᓴᐅᔪᖅ!

ᐅᓇ ᐃᓄᐃᑦ ᐅᓂᒃᑳᖓᑦ ᑲᓛᓛᑦ ᓄᓇᖓᓐᓃᙶᖅᓯᒪᔪᖅ ᐅᖃᐅᓯᖃᖅᑐᖅ ᐃᖃᓗᔅᓯᐊᕐᒥᒃ, ᐅᒃᐱᓇᓴᐅᔪᕐᒥ ᑲᑉᐱᐊᓇᖅᑐᒥᒃ ᖃᐅᔨᒪᔭᐅᑦᓗᓂ "ᐃᖃᓗᒡᔪᐊᖅ ᐃᖃᓗᒃ," ᑐᓴᐅᒪᔭᐅᔪᖅ ᓴᐳᒻᒥᑦᑎᓲᖑᓂᖓᓂᒃ ᐃᓕᐊᕐᔪᓂᒃ ᐅᐃᒡᒐᕐᓂᕐᓂᑦᓗ ᐱᕐᓕᕋᕐᓂᐊᖏᒻᒪᑦ.

ᒪᕐᕉᒃ ᐃᓕᐊᕐᔫᒃ ᕿᒪᒃᑕᐅᔪᕚᓂᒃ ᓄᓇᖅᑲᑎᖏᓐᓄᑦ ᓂᖅᑭᒃᓴᖃᖅᑎᑦᑎᔪᓐᓇᐃᓪᓕᒪᑕ. ᐊᓐᓇᒃᑐᕚᓂᒃ ᐸᐅᕐᖓᖅᑑᓴᒃᐸᒃᑐᑎᒃ ᖁᓖᓕᒐᕐᓂᒡᓗ, ᑎᒍᐊᖅᑎᒋᓚᐅᖅᑕᖓᑕ ᐱᑎᑉᐸᓐᓂᕐᒪᒋᑐᑦ, ᑭᓯᐊᓂ ᐅᑭᐅᕈᓈᖅᐳᖅ, ᐱᕐᓕᓇᐊᑭᑦᓕᑦᓗᑎᒡᓗ. ᐅᓐᓄᐊᑉ ᐃᓚᖓᓐᓂᑦ ᐱᖅᓯᖅᑐᐊᓘᑎᑦᓗᒍ, ᓂᐱᒥᒃ ᑐᓴᖅᐳᒃ ᑐᖅᓲᖕᓂ ᑕᑯᑦᓗᑎᒡᓗ ᐃᖃᓗᔅᓯᐊᕌᓗᖕᒥᒃ ᐅᖁᒻᒥᐊᖅᑐᒥᒃ ᓂᕿᒥᒃ. ᐃᖃᓗᔅᓯᐊᑉ ᓂᓇᑎᑦᑐᓂᒋᒃ ᐊᖏᕐᕋᒥᓅᖃᑎᒋᔪᒪᑦᓗᓂᒋᑦᓗ ᐅᑭᐅᓕᒫᖅ ᓂᕿᒃᓴᖃᑦᑎᐊᕐᓂᐊᕐᒪᑎᒃ ᐊᓐᓇᑦᓗᑎᒃ. ᐅᑦᓗᐃᑦ ᐃᓚᖓᓐᓂᑦ ᐃᖃᓗᔅᓯᐊᖅ ᐊᖏᕐᕋᕐᓂᙱᓚᖅ. ᐊᖑᓂᒃᑕᐅᓐᓂᕐᒪᑦ ᑯᒍᑎᓕᒃᔪᐊᕐᒧᑦ ᐊᕐᕕᕐᒧᑦ, ᓱᕈᓰᓪᓗ ᓇᓂᔭᐅᒐᒥᒃ ᑎᒍᐊᖅᑖᖑᓂᖅᐳᒃ ᐃᓚᒌᓄᑦ.

Background Photograph: © PhotoJanski/SHutterstock.com

Illustrations: Rebecca Brook

ᓴᓇᔪᐅᑎᑕᐅᓯᒪ: ᓂᐅᑦ ᑯᓂᙳᑕᖅ
ᐊᖅᑭᒃᓱᐃᔨᖏᑦ: ᒪᓂᑲ ᐃᑕᑐᒃᓯᙳᑦᐊᑦ (Inuktitut)
ᐲᑕ ᐅᐊᑦ (English)

ᐃᓅᒃᑎᑐᓕᕆᓴᒃᑎᑕᐅᓯ: ᑐᐃᔅ ᕿᒡHᐅᕻᑎ
ᑐᑭᒃᐊᑎᑕᐅᓯ: ᑕᓂ ᑯᓂᙳᑕᖅ
ᐊᖅᑭᒃᓱᐃᔨ: ᖏᒪ ᔨ

For more information please contact:
info@inhabitmedia.com

Inhabit Media Inc.
P.O.Box 11125, Iqaluit, NU, X0A 1H0

www.inhabitmedia.com

We acknowledge the support of the
Canada Council for the Arts for our publishing
program.

This project was made possible in part by the
Government of Canada.

Background photograph: © Rich Carey/Shutterrstock.com

Canadä

Canada Council   Conseil des Arts
for the Arts   du Canada

KAAKULUK

INSIDE THIS ISSUE:

Cover Illustration: Ben Shannon

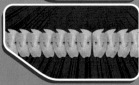
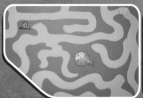

GREENLAND SHARKS?

class: chondrichthyes
(cartilaginous fishes)
species: Somniosus microcephalus
length: 2.5 to 7.3 m
weight: Up to 1,200 kg

"IT HAS SMALL TEETH AND A LOT OF FAT."
ASTA HOKANAK, KUGLUKTUK

"IT LOOKS LIKE A GIANT FISH, BUT SCARIER. THEY LOOK MEAN."
UKPIK KAYASARK, KUGAARUK

"THEY'RE REALLY BIG AND CAN BE REALLY OLD. AND THEY HAVE LOTS OF SMALL SHARP TEETH."
ARIEL DESIREE ITTIMANGNAQ, KUGAARUK

WORDS OF WISDOM

By Jaypeetee Arnakak, *Clyde River*

Clyde River

Greenland sharks can live a long time—hundreds of years. It is said that they may have the potential to live forever if they are not killed. When they are killed, their jaws will continue to bite when food is placed in them, even after the head is removed from the body.

Illustration: © Dotted Yeti/Shutterstock.com

Greenland Sharks: the mysterious "sleeper shark"!

Greenland sharks live in the waters of the Arctic Ocean off the northern coast of Baffin Island and around Greenland and Iceland, but they have been spotted as far south as Florida in the right water conditions. They usually live in very deep, very cold water (up to 2,774 m below the surface) and are rarely seen.

Predators
Greenland sharks do not have any known natural predators other than humans.

Babies
Greenland shark babies are born from eggs held within the mother's body until birth. They produce about 10 offspring at a time. Shark babies are called "pups."

Food
Greenland sharks are known to eat just about anything! They are believed to be mostly scavengers, which means they will eat the meat of dead animals that they come across—such as the carcasses of seals, fish, whales, and even polar bears and caribou.

Size

Greenland sharks are huge! They can weigh up to 1,200 kg and reach 7.3 m in length. For reference, 1,200 kg is about the weight of 15 grown men! Only the largest great white sharks can grow to be larger than a Greenland shark.

Speed

Greenland sharks have incredible speed—*incredibly slow* that is. They usually swim about 1.2 km per hour, with their fastest possible burst of speed being about 3.6 km per hour. Compare that to the great white shark's fastest recorded speed burst of approximately 40 km per hour, and you'll see how slow moving these creatures are. In fact, the Greenland shark has the lowest swim speed for its size of any fish. Their reputation for sluggishness has earned them the nickname "the sleeper shark."

Eyesight

Greenland sharks are often partially blind. A parasite commonly attaches itself to the shark's eyes, causing damage to the cornea (the outer layer of the eyeball), which leaves it partially blind. This isn't a big problem for Greenland sharks, though. Because very little light reaches the depths at which the sharks live, they don't need their eyesight to catch prey. Greenland sharks rely on their remaining senses to find prey. Some scientists believe that the parasites in the sharks' eyes actually attract prey to the sharks. The parasite that is found in Greenland sharks' eyes may be bioluminescent (meaning it produces light), which may attract other animals to the sharks.

Longevity

The Greenland shark is the longest-living vertebrate on Earth. Its lifespan is at least 272 years, and they could live up to 500 years. Because Greenland sharks are part of the class of cartilaginous fishes— aquatic animals whose skeletons are made of soft cartilage rather than hard bone—it is hard to know their exact age. Bones are easier for scientists to age than cartilage, so it is not totally clear how old Greenland sharks actually are.

TERRIFYING TEETH

TOP ROW

BOTTOM ROW

Greenland sharks have very strange teeth for a shark. On their upper jaws they have 48 to 52 pointed, thin teeth, and on their lower jaws they have about the same number of wide teeth curved outward. The top teeth hold the shark's prey in place, while the lower teeth cut a round plug of flesh for the shark to eat. In order to do this, Greenland sharks swing their heads in a circular motion while eating.

By cutting a plug of meat from its prey, the Greenland shark is able to feed on prey that would be too large for it to eat without this adaptation—like whale carcasses.

The strange teeth of the Greenland shark have earned it a mysterious reputation. When seals with wounds that wound around their bodies like a corkscrew began washing up on Sable Island, Nova Scotia, researchers wanted to find out what fearsome beast could do such damage. Some people—including *National Geographic* filmmakers—blamed the Greenland shark and dubbed the shark "The Corkscrew Killer." There is much debate over whether the Greenland shark is the culprit, but one thing is for sure: this slow-moving shark packs one strange bite!

TRADITIONAL AND MODERN USES

Greenland Shark

"Greenland sharks are not common around the South Baffin region of Nunavut, but as you go north they are caught quite regularly in fishing nets."

—**William Flaherty**, Grise Fiord, Nunavut

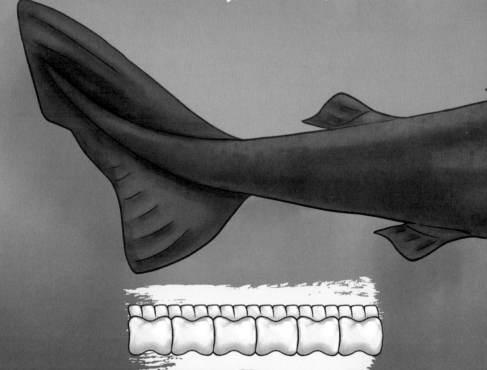

Cartilage:
- The skeleton of the Greenland shark is made from cartilage, not bone.
- Shark cartilage was traditionally wound together and used as a bouncy ball for children.

Illustrations: Rebecca Brook

Liver:
- In Greenland and Iceland, Greenland sharks were fished for their liver oil, which was used to light lamps.
- In the early 20th century, there were up to 50,000 Greenland sharks caught for this purpose every year.

Meat:
- On Baffin Island, Greenland sharks are not generally eaten or fished intentionally.
- In Greenland, they are fished and the meat is usually fed to dogs.
- In Iceland, Greenland sharks make up the national dish! The meat of the shark is fermented and hung to dry for 4 or 5 months. This dish is a delicacy in Iceland, but it tends to be very stinky!

THE AMAUTALIK

By Aviaq Johnston

Illustrated by Jazmine Gubbe

There are monsters and creatures that roam the land and sea. One of these monsters is the *amautalik*. She is a large, ugly woman who likes to steal children and put them into the basket on her back so that she can take them to her home and *EAT THEM*.

One day, the amautalik was walking throughout the land. She was searching for something, or someone, to catch because she was very hungry. Finally, she heard voices and she saw two children sitting alone with no adults around to watch them.

The two children were a boy and a girl. The boy was an orphan who lived with his grandma. Because he was an orphan, his clothes were given to him when others had outgrown them. They often did not fit him well and had many rips. You could even see his big toe poking through a hole in one of his *kamiik*!

The girl was his only friend. She was kind and enjoyed spending time with him because he always had interesting stories to tell. The boy was teased by the other kids a lot and he wasn't included in games. The boy spent a lot of time listening to elders tell stories, and he always told these stories to the girl.

He was in the middle of telling a story when the amautalik snuck up behind them. When the amautalik was close enough to grab them, her shadow fell over the children. The girl and the boy turned to see her.

The amautalik was huge and scary and stinky! The girl was sure that they were going to be taken and eaten.

The boy was scared, but he was thinking of a plan. Since he had no one to take care of him, the boy often had to think of ways to help himself out of situations.

"Shhhhh," said the boy. He pointed at his toe wiggling through the hole in his kamik. "Shh," he said again, "you'll wake it up."

The amautalik had never seen a child that wasn't scared of her before. She was confused, staring at the wiggling toe. She asked, "What is it?"

The boy kept wiggling his toe. "Shhh, it's a monster," he replied.

"What does the monster eat?" the amautalik asked, sounding a little worried.

"This monster," the boy said, "EATS *AMAUTALIIT*!"

The amautalik stumbled back a few steps. "Keep it away from me!" she yelled as she ran away.

Shark Maze!

Help this Greenland shark reach its next meal at the bottom of the ocean!

Illustration: Rebecca Brook

GREENLAND SHARKS IN MYTHOLOGY!

THIS INUIT LEGEND FROM GREENLAND TELLS THE STORY OF THE *EQALUSSUAQ*, A MYTHOLOGICAL CREATURE ALSO CALLED "THE SHARK FISH," THAT IS KNOWN TO PROTECT ORPHANS AND WIDOWS FROM STARVATION.

Two orphans were left behind at a settlement when none of the other families were able to provide for them. They survived by eating black crowberries and a little *ammassat*, which their former foster mother had given them, but soon winter came and they began to starve. One night while a snowstorm was raging, they heard a noise in the passage and a big Eqalussuaq turned up with a piece of meat in its mouth. Eqalussuaq fed them and told them to come with it to its house where it had enough food for them to survive the winter. One day the Eqalussuaq didn't come home. It had been hunted and eaten by a sperm whale, but the children were found and adopted by a new family.

Publisher: Neil Christopher
Editors: Monica Ittusardjuat (Inuktitut)
                Kelly Ward (English)
Translator: Louise Flaherty
Art Director: Danny Christopher
Designer: Sam Tse

_____

For more information please contact:
info@inhabitmedia.com

Inhabit Media Inc.
P.O. Box 11125, Iqaluit, NU, X0A 1H0

www.inhabitmedia.com

We acknowledge the support of the
Canada Council for the Arts for our publishing
program.

This project was made possible in part by the
Government of Canada.

Canadä

Canada Council   Conseil des Arts
for the Arts   du Canada